I0192805

Some for Humor, Some for Verse, Some for Longing, Some for Terse

Second Edition

Poems and Pictures from

Steven C. Ihde

Why a second edition? Poetry is not stagnant. This writer revisits work and sees with changed eyes. While the titles are the same, the poems have been edited and consequently read differently than the first edition. Is this significant? The author thinks so. It is hoped that more clarity is an outcome. In this edition there are numerous full stops, some longer pauses, and many lines rush to the next and farther. Pace for this writer is important, and is a significant reason why the new edition is made.

Poems   *page*

3

Poems   *page*

Heartbeats

Like syncopated rhythm of kindred heartbeats,
Channels cutting granite face of El Capitan,
Give message to rock climbers, hanging without net,
Pinions extended as elbows scream, is it yet,
Too late to turn back, to relent, is this last stand,
As winds whipping from west, upriver in streaks,

Gathers her forces, repelling adulterers,
Who have no rightful claim to this face they defame,
Chisel and clamp, clarions scarring their progress,
Markers in contrast to runoffs, needing egress,
Bridging peaceful valley, glacial remnant remains,
Firm against onslaught of two foolish foreigners,

Twins yet not true sisters, await on valley floor,
Casting fitful incantations to ward off the pall,
Gripping loins as climbers fingers had explored,
Now wrenching in agony where had been enjoyed,
The night of preparation before this great wall,
Whose face calls in challenge to come open the door,

To reach through the heavens, to challenge the unknown,

5

Where no right-minded citizen would here select,
Such pathways to glory, so deadly is the choice,
A crack in granite cliff belies valley's true voice,
This Yosemite, no friend, she is not direct,
Will swallow without remorse, without remorse shown,

What regrets have mountains that have resisted time,
Much worse than such chisel has cut them through ages,
Softer than goose down is the touch of these footfalls,
As scalers rappel in retreat, their conquest calls,
For wisdom to prevail as wind whips their stages,
Who like irritant fleas on their carcasses dine,

Give me men to conquer these mountains is the cry,
And women to cringe at doorstep as they await,
Or women to bray as hellhounds into the fray,
Distress heathen concubines who sob in dismay,
Take shield and buckler just as climbers do belay,
Wreak carnage on El Capitan of starlit sky,

Would heartbeats sway to other song if they could hear,
Would climbers repent of damage done to stone face,
Would annals record the actions of men who tried,
Would songs be sung, legends written of those who died,

Would deeds be lost and forgotten, leaving no trace,
When howling winds no more blow, and rain sheds no tear.

In the Lane

In a lane to skip, to construct a fantasy,
Under mist endowed branches dripping over me.
In mid afternoon hours I plumb the depths here,
I search for the muses to transport the seer.

Are they under these stones or hiding in this bush
So covered with moss and grey mushrooms in a rush?
To make known their presence with lichen they submit
A fell fragrance to capture such dreams as see fit.

The dryads and naiads wait so patiently here.
Their wiles will be strong and Alcinoe I hear.
Her soft voice in whisper beckons to me this day,
Echoed with Meliae of the ash trees who say

Come closer the pathway that leads to our glen sweet,
We offer rich rewards, for such seekers we greet
Under the spell that we have invited you now
To share in our heritage under this sweet bough.

Partake of our promise and rejoice this day.
Our riches from fountain and deep roots we display.

To each who would seek to more deeply be inspired,
Open heart and desire are what are required,

Freely we offer, do not delay nor dawdle
There on the verge as you gaze into that puddle.
For we wait to transport you to another place
Where fantasy is real that lights every face.

Madame Georges

Madame Georges manages her household,
Making bed linens, crewel comforters,
Mending pillow cases with silk threads.
Masters her craft as ship's captain will
Wager his crew, uses to challenge
Wrestling with wind filling full all sails
While Madam Georges waits on widow's walk.
Watching the tide roll in peacefully,
Wanting her woeful man to return.
Will he sail safely atop high seas,
Where gales whip round Tierra Fuego,
When whalers seek white monster of deep?

Whispers fill deck between those on watch.
Wary, their captain watches some spume,
Willing that whale to rise and show forth.
Wasted his musings, for far away
White monster cleaves waves, breaching freed floe,
Waking the demons resting on beds
Where have been banished, Neptune decreed.
Willful their actions raised banishment.
Marauders they were, setting themselves

10

Masters of oceans as was their wont.
Misplaced their affections, filled with pride.
Made idols of worship and bowed down.

Misplaced were attentions, so Neptune
Masked them with starfish, clung to their forms.
Making them crawl among sea worms, bred
Monstrous creatures to churn briny deep.
Where foolish captains take ships to hunt
White beasts whose horns will puncture their keels.
Whose malice is known by these hunters
When in northern waters ply their trade.
Where sailed that captain, seeking monster
Who taunts his thoughts, ransacking such peace,
Wherewith he could comfort appetite
With fresh fish, not mammal, which he seeks.

Winter is not kind to those on sea,
Whipping resistance, wresting away
What hope had carried men from home,
While those left alone on widow's walks
Weep for the lost carried under waves.
Waves that were not friendly, Atlantic
Wantonly and irreverently

Wrapped them in shrouds of white capped regions.
Pall bearers swept ships downward to beds,
Poseidon did welcome arrivals.
Plaudits he fully heaped on their heads.
Perhaps they would rue such dark welcome.

Perhaps they gave voice, their destruction
Prompted some repentance, some action
Proper to present situation.
Perhaps they would cry out, yet too late
Were words of pleadings, when no mercy
Would greet their appearance, while the throes
Whip through their corpses, enlivening
White beasts to feast on seamen's bodies
Who hunted in former days on sea.
While watching and waiting far away
Widows do weep next to Madame Georges,
Wringing their hands with linens she made.

Witness the comfort they gain from her,
With crewel embroidered names she plies them,
William and Winston, Warner and Shawn
Will never return, for under waves

Will they lie in rest so far from home.
Welcomed by Poseidon, Neptune known
Written in annals, in Roman climes,
Worshipped as sea god by fishermen
Making their way across Middle Sea,
Malta gave refuge ere Marausa,
Making men hope, false was their slumber,
Met swift demise with all hands on board.

Mesdames have often awaited their men.
Mademoiselles dream one comes along.
Madame Georges manages household skills,
Making bed linens, crewel comforters,
Wrestling her demons, weeping her pain.
Wrapped in her sorrow, never again
Will welcome home husband, this she knows,
Who sailed far in his search for white whales.
Warriors they were, fighting each other,
Where waves, deep and mighty swept away
What hopes they carried in cold waters,
Would never return to Frankish shores.

Stones

Wading along lake shore,
Searching for stones to throw,
Two are one in purpose here,
Clasping hands, do endear,
Words between unneeded,
Each to other ceded,
Signing pact, intertwined,
Not with ink, one of mind,
As stones are uplifted,
To each other are gifted,
Held against beating heart,
Signifying fresh start,
At this shore many tears,
Sink with stones, taking fears.

Guardians

Boundary, barrier high, between San Andreas, arid to bone-
dry
and land to west, bears pinyon, clinging to harsh cliffside,
marks dominion.

Ancient guards, neighbors for years, speak not to each
other, share not the tears.
Unmovable, set in ways, continue in silence, number their
days.

Witness all, sunshine and rain, seasons bring buffeting, so
hurt by strain.
One clings to earth, reaching deep, while other was sky
born, from heaven's keep.

Deeply pitted, crystalized veins, instructed by Ares,
harboring pain.
Warrior steeled, firm entrenched, so stalwart in hard times,
will not be wrenched.

Holds hilltop against all odds, holds foes in contempt,
yields not to prods

brought against him, untold years. Myriad heathens tried,
yet shed no tears.

Like watchman full duty bound, diligent in duty, like
guarding hound
grips intruders, won't release, deep craggy wounds inflicts,
without surcease.

When came joy, there was surprise, foundations were still
firm, ended were lies.
Laid down their swords, achieved their best, their duties are
fulfilled, have received their rest.

Joy

Archangels shall be fully satisfied,
Ministry to the heirs,

With word promised to betrothed not yet bride,
One who would take all tears.

To carry announcements of revealed plan
To men's and women's ears,

Received, yet not seen, not since time began,
By those so blessed to hear.

As watching over flock when appeared sight,
Shining bright as to blind,

The messengers shared news of that night,
Joyous for all mankind,

Restoration for all, for all who should
Receive the gift refined,

As by prophet's word, the one who came would

17

Fulfill all as designed,

Made to conform to all that's good and blessed,
Opening the garden

Where bliss is record of each breath we take,
Where nothing does harden.

The soul of man nor woman will not break,
Where each receives pardon.

No longer flaming sword will guard the gate
East of fairest Eden.

Heavenly messengers shall all assuage,
For accuser meets judge.

The prime deceiver he did discourage,
Since that morning where smudge,

The image held reflection of glory,
Yet replaced was courage.

And jealousy proclaimed a sad story,

18

Not sweet as would borage

With taste of bee honey, such starry blooms,
Blue in color profound

Are like the promise on lips of all grooms,
To be gentle and sound,

To share daily faithfulness in all rooms,
To never bring to ground.

To have and hold, in gentleness or glooms,
That may happen around,

Whether in meadow or torrential rain,
Where this couple is paired.

Where peaceful melody relieves the strain,
Of what daily impaired.

Or agony is great and as storm clouds rage,
To what is this compared?

Such pouring tears are wept, we may not gauge,

The dark depth they each shared.

Still, beyond this picture assembled stand,
A gathering in light.
Witnesses of fulfilled promise in new land,
Land where light is so bright.

Whose source of life is from eternity,
And this life has been shared.

We may now face death with sanguinity,
For one who died so dared

Take all of the burden that on us fell,
For he for us has cared.

On Golgotha he took payment for Hell
So that we might be spared.

Prophets of old have their visions revealed,
Glorious will be end.

What heard from the messengers was concealed
Who would be one to mend.

With visions glorious how would be healed,
How could such men attend.

Beyond understanding were images,
What would happen at end.

Close up the book until time all fulfill,
Nothing to it added.

As shepherds who witnessed that night on hill,
As pillows are padded.

Such comfort received for good news did hear,
As messengers said,

Peace on earth, good will to all who draw near,
Here is life giving bread.

And such company joined to fill that sky,
Light was like a new day.

Like timpani struck to record on high,
Death no longer has sway.

The voices in chorus so glorious,
To all who did betray,

Who should have fled demon notorious,
Who dead in sin did lay.

Such message is to these hearers so sweet,
Like fresh dew on flowers,

Grants life for the day where light so complete,
Will renew, empowers.

And welcome is such great restoration,
That angels recount hours

They long waited to witness salvation
That is so freely ours.

Venus

Elegant as Florentine marble,
Honed and polished to purest sheen,
With clarity of crystal structure,
Without price in estimation.

On a proscenium constructed,
Thirty meters by seventeen,
Surmounted by Hera's three graces,
Her bloom and joyfulness is known.

Even the sun for brightness falls short
When on platform her grace reveals.
A peacock fans large for attention.
She needs no such ornate display.

Her smile melts hopeful hearts like butter.
Her heart is her own and stone cold.

Conductor

Crescent light does glower, quartered, in black,
as cicada concert, crescendo rising,
took pause, caught breath, turning nature' clock back.
High dungeoned moon, behind cloud retreating
scowls in silence, for whom ears do attune.
Greater numbers indignant, yet shall the mass
across void universe, measure a spoon
that doles out by portion, what comes to pass:
Who edits each season written out
from ebony as sliver emerges.
Conceiving symphony, cicadas shout,
unable to suppress orb-sent urges.
Though moon we do not hear, cicadas fear
orchestra conductor, in spring of year.

Huntress

Baleful butterfly, deftly to flower,
antenna aware, avoids predation.
From chrysalis torn, in summer shower,
like Indian cat, black stripe construction.

Hidden in shadows, tall savannah grass
blends with fell hunter, no flower aware
danger approaches, gasps not out "alas."
Nectar thievery, shall swift come to pass.

Death stalks each flower, harsh as striped tiger,
who from hunger hunts, and scenting the prey,
lands lightly atop, like feral fighter,
in grasslands is king, all others give way.

Tiger swallowtail, so apt is the name.
Without affection, brings end to its game.

At Edge

On the windowsill of desperation,
where the cracking ice is at point of thaw,
before the drop into oblivion,
at cusp of nightmare, where death opens maw,

Could I your colors savor, light a balm,
each ray bring prosperity to this life,
morning, afternoon, and evening calm,
then enter the night without fear of strife,

The prescription, this hour available,
not from pharmacist, yet one winsome smile,
will cross chasms, break grim grip, capable,
assuaging my airwaves, tuned to new dial,

So crisp, my stereo receiver band,
your runes, kite magic, inscribing my hand.

Love's Pyre

Pile higher the kindling, the match you hold,
prepared for this moment, ready to strike.
we are combination, ice, water cold,
becomes vapor with you, and so alike.

Flames licking my ankles, this is my pyre,
freely sap is flowing, freed by her heat.
her fingers tantalize, tickling desire,
willingly I suffer, I am complete.

an offering prepared, cut me to quick,
torture endure, gladly endure, torture of mind.
your hold on me is such, heart being sick,
emotions running wild, we are entwined.

Eros seldom refused, who strikes with dart,
we desire his arrows, that is his art.

Lacking Tan

Jolly man who has no tan, as a clam
seeking solitude from passing seagulls,
digs deeper, buries himself in hot sand:
finding relief from life's incessant turmoils.

With neck protruding to greatest extent
he's discovering barnacles attached.
so long as he lain, no way to prevent,
such suckers from feeding where have latched
onto fairest skin, so soft and compliant.
For these beasts he's a veritable feast,
like Gulliver traveling, this giant
is captured by creatures, who are the least
in kingdom, this phylum Arthropoda,
plays havoc on him, music sans coda.

South of Horn

We are on the threshold, the dice we roll,
a ribbed track to follow, that weaves and winds.
Pitfalls, scree washes share, planted is pole.
Ribbon marks accident, are we these kinds?

Adventurers, ones who risk lives, shall we,
irrespective, though adrenaline drains,
climb? "Caution is for cowards, we won't be
so influenced," he quivers, she claims.

First foot forward, though albatross hangs dead,
impaled on pole, carrying curse to all.
We were never sailors, portent not read.
Had neither known ocean, nor heeded call.

So grievous path chosen, consumed, can't change.
No help is coming, out of cell phone range.

Where Time Yearns

In this land where time turns backwards,
Where twice bloomed blossoms reverse to seed,
Clouds drain upwards each afternoon,
Winds sup up the air we so need.

Songs are sung before are written,
Our ears do hear a memory,
It is ether in our bloodstream,
Gaseous realm aiding to see.

Our inner eye reveals secrets,
Inside this brain images call,
Coyote mending buffalo,
Roaming the ancient kingdom's hall.

That isle in visions appearing,
Where boundaries are yet unknown,
When waters dwell above heavens,
Where angels' morn, brightly shone.

Nascent dawn of whole creation,
When elements are not existing,

Comes a spark, a word is spoken,
And since that time still persisting.

As perpetual machine hums,
As unwound clock ever ticking,
All energy does not fade away,
Like spring uncoiled remains springing.

In this time made of elements,
And elements simply transform,
What is today is memory,
Time turned on ear is all have known.

Puce and Pink

Puce and pink wearily wilt in unseasonable heat.
Under burden, willow and plum, crocus and vinca,
are crushed in the hands of weather's assault.
Each and all plead cease of storms.

Weeps the sky, weeps the willow,
while plum struggles to remain in blossom,
while crocus sadly collapses beneath burden,
yet vinca, deeply grasping hillside, is not troubled,
while each gust bodes neighbors' efforts are in vain.

As plum petals form thickening mattress,
air is sanctified with fragrant oil,
as petals flutter, broken from grip with each draft,
separated messengers remind us life is fleeting.

Birth is tormented, renewal requires sacrifice,
though pangs seem silent, the aware ear
yet may discern their conversations
whispered on the soughing breezes,
shouted between storm tossed stones.

As the natural world responds,
as the interactions continue unabated,
as richness mounts higher, deeper,
forming stronger relationships

It is for us to discover,
daily transference of energies,
commerce between root and plant,
what results from weeping and resisting,
torment and sacrifice, death and birth.

Puce and pink, announcers of agony,
wearily wait, while gasping last breaths,
yet agony brings another life,
and another, and another.

Chain

Knowing not where this path leads me,
My steps are not taken lightly.
Like a gauntlet with fearful blows,
Like a taut wire where stay on toes,
As wind catches up the dry leaf
Where people may lose their belief,
In trepidation I must go
As knees buckle, begins the snow.

Such portent, like evil eye know,
Like red sky at morning will show
Sailors their destiny of grief,
So wind they up their mourning sheets,
Preparing for mortal death throes
When hear crows nest cry "Thar she blows!"
Put backs into oars so strongly,
Death soon rakes in buckets brightly.

Red swirls around my feet, leads me.
In dream like trance I tread lightly.
My path now white and crimson shows
What can't be hidden in these throes

Of fear, I quake, a fallen leaf,
One who forfeited all belief.
In trepidation I do know,
This path becomes last act I know.

As glance back, the fresh fallen snow
Now hides the tracks, deep down below
The blood I shed on waves at sea,
With hands, I swear, forlorn to see
The misery I brought I know
Must be repaid before I go.
This chain I forged shall never free,
Or give respite to one like me.

Stolen Kiss

Longing is a preferred selection for the heart,
tingling is a welcomed sensation for the soul,
awaiting is a bargaining chip held in your roll,
played at the proper moment gives beneficial start.

Pleasant are formative thoughts as they do impart
hope that uplifts the spirit like a farandole,
joining hands in a lively dance, careful to control,
winding in and out like a chain before come apart.

Similarly flickers flit between branches, dart
Up then down, and north then south, is this to cajole,
like dance of courtship, with fluttering wing, is this goal
widespread across animal kingdom, a worthy art,

As when bees dip selves in flowers, doing their part
to prepare the blossom for summer season role,
are they aware their simple action will so console
twined hearts once broken apart, an upset apple cart

Spreads mayhem in village square, like blackberry tart,

though sweet in mouth, drips down your cheek, just as you stole
a kiss from redwood lips, like lumberjack climbing pole
you clambered close, then set your mark, hoping for fresh start.

Yet what was sought in anticipation, your part
became twice worse when fulfillment became the whole,
for slap you received brought you to grieve thinking that goal
was better achieved, not longing perceived, at the start.

Dead Apple

Of what harm is the apple tree,
though long dead and woodpecker
riddled, horizontal rows,
evidence of insects, ants,
whatever else is diet,
of the red head, she flashes,
drifts, a shallow arc in flight,
to perch and listen, to rat-
a-tat-a-tat-a-tat, tat,
Food for the day, food for night,
which is preferable wood?
apple or pine, not Douglas,
for his crust requires long bill.
pileated meets challenge,
yet he steers clear of apple.
is it out of some respect?
do avians recognize,
this tree for me, that for you?
what is their society>
are there fundamental rules,
governing animal kingdom?
will apple tree speak to me,

plead to not fell it today?
yet, my language confuses,
for to me dead tree is dead.
I disregard it as life source.
this apple is an eyesore.
what care I it is life source?
I hew down what bears no grudge:
tree bears no hatred towards me.
that which was beneficial,
a fountain of forest peals,
rat-a-tat, rat-a-tat, gone,
no more tree, what was the harm?

Silhouettes

Silhouettes echoed on the wall,
Reminiscences of life last Autumn.
Cumulous clouds thrusted so tall,
Skylark, sang warning, of my pall.

White heather called me back in thrall,
Prisoner of highland's bogs at bottom.
Ben Nevis rose higher than all,
Loch Lomond draped in dark shawl.

Animosity rankled gall,
Fearful I trod towards printed erratum.
Caught in quagmire, what shall befall,
I saw no benefit at all.

Curses spoken refused to fall.
Misspent youth, under ceilidh music thrum,
Death stick, gasper, would end it all:
Coughing up lungs, punched as by awl.

Grasping silhouettes are not small.
Rhythmic, they dance, as dark ancient totem

reared over my head in this hall
challenged each witness to recall.

Was ever required payment's call?
pawnbroker of souls beats ponderous drum.
darkness is come, there is no stall.
shroud surrounds me in this death hall.

From up out my coffin I call.
My words fall, unanswered, no one shall come.
Too late, for I have paid out all.
All that remains is my fire fall.

John and Orion

On rolling prairie to south of Moore,
John Ware sets out a general store,
Not far from creek crossing dirt pathway,
Low lying in gulley to this day,
Yet long gone is the store of John Ware,
No soul living today gives a care.

What concern is John, so far long gone,
More like a feather than bristlecone,
Slight as sassafras twig in springtime,
Yet tough as wolverine in his prime.
Hands scarred as are arms since fatal fire,
That took away his one heart's desire.

Good enough as any for goodbyes,
How many pennies will pay for lies,
If pennies are thoughts, there were too few,
Like barren landscape, everyone knew,
There was no more water he could draw,
His bag gave up last drop, so he saw

Horizons held his one salvation,

And like so many crossed the nation.
With heart as his fist so firmly clenched,
Like mustang mare in prairie entrenched,
Would not be driven, tests his mettle,
through harsh winters where did settle.

Once all in the county, wagoned bands,
Left ruts digging deeply in grasslands.
A journey begun from crack of dawn,
When stars low in sky, Orion's arm
Dangles near belt, withered are his hands
Since crushed while a youth in the Badlands,

Spoke split under weight when struck a stone,
And standing too close took with it bone
Of arm pushing wheel over that rock.
Too late is outcry, too quick the shock.
Ton of goods brought resulted in groan.
Since that spring day Orion does moan.

Moans for the mornings of Michigan,
Recalls the joys before he was ten,
Hanging from low oak over stream bed,
Dipping his feet, then dipping his head.

43

Waters ran deep, every now and then,
A trout would appear, and bring a grin.

Brown was his side, as brown as the hair,
Curling as corkscrews in summer air.
Dusted with plum pollen floating low,
Rejoicing with birdsongs he did know,
Meadowlark trill, or whippoorwill there,
Whose chirp chirp warned of cougar or bear.

Not myth I relate, not tall, but true,
Fills Montana skies, so wide, so blue.
John Ware and Orion crossed the veil,
Sad there are few give credence to tale.
It takes more than thoughts, matters not who,
Will write down records of people knew.

In Foreign Beds

So often sleeping in a foreign bed,
Visions of that dark Mary, like a blight,
ill at ease and cold, I tremble all night,
Hoping somehow, this vision could be shed.

I hear her dire command enter my head.
I feel her cold fingers, like death's delight.
I succumb to the vision, such my plight.
I tremble and twitch, throw covers off bed.

Having no recourse, by vision am led,
Itching at my side, sustains me in fright.
Viscous floor hinders, I search for a light.
Searching is useless, in land of the dead.

I touch with my foot, toes digging instead,
I shelter not back, much craving some sight.
I come to that bump, I sense some delight,
I hear the bump thump, my heart rules my head.

Such vision contorts, my eyes scale my head,
Victory cedes to dark Mary. In fright
I stagger backwards from that ghastly sight,
Hoping against hope, this vision is shed.

In thrall so passes each desperate bed.
I crave surcease, yet continues more fright.

45

I'm trapped in this quagmire every night.
In sweat soaked clothing I shiver in dread.

Hatching a plea, torn from my hairless head,
Incumbent upon me, need for delight,
Veins pulsate blood, then see I the light,
Saving morning has come, gone are the dead.

I must face the next sorrow, what I dread.
I travel all day to reach the next site.
I seek for warm bed, though none are in sight.
I fear same vision will enter my bed.

Suffering with malaise I lay down in bed.
Victim of mad Mary, not my delight.
Intentions are fruitless, imprisoned my sight.
Heavenly deliverance frees my head.

In spite of ignominy, I, instead,
In rejuvenated life, rising height,
Incensed, yet inspired, grows my candlelight.
I escape this vision, escape this dread.

Restart

If I perspire while sitting close to you,
If my temperature rises a degree or two,
If my eyes bulge or ears begin to ring,
Do not take alarm, it's only a minor thing.

I say it's only minor, for you affect me so,
My blood pressure rises, and I begin to glow
At the slightest torment to this weak heart,
And your presence is torment from the start.

Please do not speak, for I shall surely quail,
My knees will break and buckle, and I may turn tail,
Retreat back to shell, back to my cocoon,
A chrysalis form again, protecting from doom,

From birds of prey, whose talons dig so deep,
and whose sharp beaks break through my much practiced
techniques,
The facade I erect for protection
Collapses so quickly with my indecision.

For when I would raise my voice and would speak,

My throat constricts tightly resulting in mouse squeak.
My message to you is swallowed in whole,
So retreat back to safety as in ferret's hole

Dug for myself for such moments as these.
It's better to be prepared than holding the cheese.
Better to escape the trap set for me,
I see the trouble and like house mouse I must flee.

So why do I approach you may well ask
If such an encounter brings terror as clown mask
Is feared by many children, scaring them,
Giving them scream-filled nightmares, creating mayhem,

Parents must run from tent with them in tow,
Embarrassed and ashamed of why they left the show
That all others enjoyed, who laughed so hard,
Their bellies shook as jelly when they dropped their guard.

Yet, guarded am I, can do no other,
I've twice been burnt by love, it is such a bother
To try to trust again, to give my heart.
Please be patient with me as I seek to restart.

Perspiration will bead across my brow,
My tongue will get twisted as does escape a growl.
I'm not angry with you, it's my own fault.
I will surely stammer my words, should call a halt

And get down on my knees, this ring proffer,
To find place on darling finger is my offer.
No words can I find, your smile's all I need.
You've truly captured this heart, I'm captured indeed.

Breaking Hearts

Moon of night, harboring deep shadows,
quaking hearts do wonder, what is slight,

May the intentional, or the fault,
go to bed, be inconsequential,

Or again, rear terrifying head,
rashly and ruinous, snuff the light,

Dampen beyond relief, stub the wick,
drowning life, as puddling wax does form,

So burdened, overcome and broken,
footfalls may continue, or feet fail,

Such weak light, crouching beyond clear view,
appearing first near moon, darkness breaks,

Partial orb, like scattered glass fragments,
has echo following, a shadow,

Like an echo rebounds, passing source,

releasing, an echo, a measure

Does reveal spirit of passing sphere,
messenger of mid night, pocked and scarred,

Repercussions of acts rashly done,
the wrong truths, released before rehearsed

Brought damage, irreparable harm,
one part to the other, falling parts,

Rending from crystal form, each segment,
each small part, essential for total,

Squandered heap, mounding much heavier,
hiding all essential, then weak light

Flickering as shadow, crouching near,
in dark breaks, a bleak full measured moon.

Mist

Morning mists, like dreams of night, provide some respite.
Calming were my thoughts as gentle light broke the night.

With eyes as fog filled like enclosed sea and islands,
With mind as muddled like sea weeds clinging to sands,

This day, with joy or sadness, hidden as in fog,
Or brighter ray will break through, calling off the dog.

So settle I in, ever enwrapped in covers.
Some warmth I do seek, or some respite from bothers.

Protection providing, though fragile as feather,
Ensconced I will remain, even if would rather,

Break out of this doldrum, I am yet unable,
My vision stays clouded, my thoughts do unsettle,

Yearning brings turmoil, dreams of night do not suffice,
While this mourning mist hangs heavy over my life.

Life's Parachutes

Swimming on breeze, uplifted seedling, powered
parachute, scans the land below,
seeking worthy home, beneficial site, knowing her purpose,
and confident

that with success, will sustain frail breed, mitochondrial,
despite summer snow,
so unseasonal, in early July, worrisome weather, not heaven
sent.

so pulled up shop, burst from casing, turned face against
east, seeking south seas to know,
consummate climate, Capricorn concern, soughing breezes
join, and so have lent

some assistance, some glow burgeoning, reflection of
strength, lifts as afterglow,
just as setting sun, crosses horizon, bringing fire to sea,
raising the scent

thrown by floating weed, seeking summer beach, bobs and
shouts as bulbs, catching friendly flow,

53

from southern current, who drawn by cold clime, attract
opposites, such is the bent.

each elemental, interacts for one, seeks for earth balance,
seeks some glory show,
a knowledge so clean, devoid of disuse, reclaim symmetry,
no longer rent.

no longer harsh torn, now is forgiven, original sin, covered
as with snow.
cleansed as with hyssop, each life bearing seed, seeks a set
purpose, seeking assent

to join creation, unleash life within, sing creation's song,
not die in woe,
rather bring offspring, similar in kind, continue the species,
on continent.

Green Onions

A sneeze alters my green onion, being sliced on maple
board.
There is no other alternative, I cleanse my chosen hoard.
So poor are my germ defenses, there is no room for error.

In preparing for my meal the colander is scrubbed to shine.
The paring knife is three times sharpened, and then once
more in brine
That blade is doused in antiseptic bath, to quell the terror,

I know each time I prepare some food, so tenuous is life.
Restrictive are my boundaries, for I wish to know less
strife.
When trials come, are they fast friends, for trials do not
care for

Who they trample, or what reaction proceeds, frothy or
pure,
The dross to drain, the gold refine, clear as crystal to
secure.
I seek result to cleanse my life, so refinements I restore.

My scars are many, deeper than dermal, memories don't lie.
Physicians prescribed me medicines, here's hoping I don't die
One day too soon, or one day too late, some day I'll open door,

To cross the threshold, draw curtain back, give the last hurrah.
Yet not today, from a poisoned meal, made on onion board:
So start again with new onion, green, one onion less in hoard.

Simple as Sand

Accommodating sand, accepting our impressions,
traces of our passage, each grain cooperating,
configuration holds, while tide recedes with fair moon.

How her arc in heavens, with astrolabe confessions,
our latitude reveals, and though she is rotating,
inconsistent, yet true, like our passage this mid June.

Six nights and days shall come, each not for our possession,
yet each we strive to grasp, hours taken, no abating,
marching ever onward, while employing this lagoon.

Eight meters beyond beach, half sunken or half revealed,
unfamiliar in shape, denser grains now lay beneath,
footfalls diminishing, encrusting covers life's form.

It appears that left hand, beneath shifting sands concealed
would confess right's mirror, yet is held as in a sheath,
thus, being weighted down, atop sits massive cairngorm.

Have we treasure buried, in zeal, is armor or shield
conferred in resting place, hidden in haste beneath heath,

eternal remembrance, where is neither moth more worm?

These select impressions, sought out or as expressions
of our uncertainty, anecdotes of our dating,
we draw from precious hoard, yet never a night too soon.

With instrument measure, abacus quarter sections,
ocean pearls together, revealing, more than weighting,
we recollect the time, the hours given, and our tune

Sung melodiously, while we made the connections,
akin to grains of sand, since eons past seek mating,
passage in music held, yet shall we be bane or boon?

Target

Weeps this heart, rapt target, for her arrows,
Feathered with peacock eyes, violet blue,
Dart in flight, circling, hunting their object.

With gauze, single layered, covering shame,
Moist eyes flutter, lament tempts, to submit,
Submit, poor measured, as cracked tablespoon.

Twice tested, like tuning tine, first rang true,
Second time snapped mettle, as split did reveal,
There was no soundness, releasing grey dross.

This heart, in her smelter, is reticent.
Ever alchemist, experimenting,
Serrating his valves, seeking the measure.

A huntress is kinder, lets quarry sleep.
Lets weary prey recover in burrows,
As spoor cools and dries, faint is her object,

Whose heart weeps, fretful in uncertainty.
Where black is the moon, Lyra composing

Lamentable lyrics, burdensome lays,

Anxious is rapt target, so uncertain.
Would venture, if calmer, a word to speak.
Cradles ribs, preventing hope from rising.

Such paltry protection, flimsy cheesecloth
That separates pith and juice, love and loss,
Fall left and right, substance crumbles, target.

Poor clay mixed with water, wasted as mud,
While potter's wheel spins, hands too weak to mold,
Failed shaping the cup to catch any love.

Ode to Love

Shall this verse suffice for the night?
Are these words written down aright?
May ear and eye capture this sight?

Attuned to the universal,
Stirrup and anvil rehearsal,
Bouncing off drum, as eternal,

That mallet against skin drawn taut,
With bolder stroke the beat is brought,
Striking in syncopated thought,

A timpani firm adjusted,
Such reverberation trusted,
To echo strongly when thrusted,

Rat tat, tat a tat, rat a tat,
Like raindrops on tin roof do splat,
Harbingers of great hailstorm that

Pounds and pummels as fighter's fist,
Bloodies vision and rarely missed,

Targeted object, pounds as grist.

While may a night suffer such pain,
Renewed shall spirit be to strain,
Through another morning of rain,

And in midst of storm does reveal
Strength of purpose, and so does heal
Over scars where bruises weal.

Reminders to the lovelorn heart,
How in courage they did depart
From lawless-land upon that cart.

Two wheels drawn by a piebald mare,
No carriage holding poorer pair
Was ever seen at county fair.

With naught but torn clothes on there backs,
A few crusts of bread in their sacks,
Sought roads barely shown by the tracks

Left by wanderer long passed by
Who trekked each day carrying sigh,

A burden borne as reached toward sky.

Through toil he labored seeking fruit,
Both crisp and juicy, no dispute
Arose in thought in his pursuit

Of passion and with such intense
Ardor he sought a higher sense,
Where satisfaction should commence.

Yet satisfaction did not rise,
For in his heart he could not prise
A word to satisfy his eyes.

Such vision he unable knew,
Yet still endeavored he to view
Some light in shadow, to tell who

Would on horizon soon appear,
The one to whom he could draw near,
To bear a burden, shed a tear.

To lay by side and comfort give,
To share a crust and with him live,

63

Such a vision would sure forgive

The cruel deeds he had inflicted,
Myriad souls had restricted,
Repaid in pain, had he gifted

Each penal blessing, had so ground
Beneath his heel, in judgment bound
Any poor soul who he had found

Within the realm where he did reign.
And on each shoulder he would deign
Some infliction of gruesome pain,

In pride so ruled and struck all down,
Believing such was right of crown,
And so destroyed his wondrous town

That had once shone bright on a hill,
Was sought by all, and even still,
Is recounted by those who will

Hold high the standard of love lost,
Count as minor the greatest cost,

Though death may come, like frozen frost

Covers earth in depths of winter,
And all commerce shall so hinder,
Break like old wood, and so splinter

Into fragments that cut to quick,
Bringing blood forth, as that stick
Stabs down to heart, making it sick

Of love that had once held the sway,
Of love torn hearts which on this day,
Awoke in earnest to join the fray.

Threw off the masks and coverings,
Brought out the swords and with them swings,
Against all terror, tumult brings

To dark kingdoms that would resist,
Brightening light will not desist,
Will so triumph, break through the list

Like champions bold of renown,
Who captured strongholds, freed each town,

From wicked rulers, brought each down.

So broad rejoicing spreads in land.
Evil forgotten, all is grand.
Life, as originally planned,

Where such light does far and wide spread,
Lifts all spirits, raises the dead
Who slept in darkness, under dread.

Within that kingdom evil ruled,
Who before the gates was withstood,
By brighter angel who whole-souled

Devoted self, in service gave,
Through humble actions those who crave
To know forgiveness, so to save

From sure destruction, light to know,
Reflecting power from the glow
Of brightest Heaven that does show

In pure response, in great glory,
Primal festive, such is story,

Eden known, not allegory.

Does this reflection clear appear?
May this poet draw closer, near,
Certain of muse's message dear?

Heed such missives as are given,
Whose content scolds, now arisen,
Reveals the error of this vision?

Shall eyes behold or is hidden,
The message as it is given,
Borne on a horse rashly ridden?

Such steed is swift, does not falter,
Through desert flies, and the halter
Does not restrict, nor does alter

Course on prairie, across the wide
Expanse of land, before the tide
Sweeps over from blue oceans wide.

Yet at this moment comes a sound
As if far beneath the ground,

Rise such phantoms that do surround.

Encircles horse that ran so swift.
Grabs the bridle, as if to lift
A burden to bestow, a gift.

Yet the gift was not for freedom,
But to enslave, and be ridden
To a paddock, where was hidden

Such snares and traps of dark design,
Where the foes of light did refine
Such intents to discourage spine.

And so that steed was sorely used,
And even though she had refused,
To fall beneath, her neck was bruised.

This Arabian, not as seems,
Rent and hobbled, and so she screams,
So writhes in terror near the streams

Of Avalon where healing comes,
On coast where boulders thick with foams

Birthed by debris and flotsam forms.

Stones to withstand such storm blown waves
That in crescendo through the days
Crash unending, their trumpets raise.

Battle lines drawn, sea against shore,
Poseid and Atlas seeking more
In their struggle to break down door.

Barrier between life and death,
Who thinking some nocturnal breath
Has power to wake Elizabeth

Who is heard behind London doors,
Her ghost may wander over shores,
Is seen by poets she ignores.

Beneath her standing such do pine.
Her collar stiffened, red with wine,
She spilled in death, setting a sign

To signify anger she bore
Against that William, he who tore

Her heart with love lost evermore.

Created in tale of Romeo
Who shared with lovers here below,
Such weakness in resolve did show

While seeking through another's dream,
Whose moon diminished, made it seem
His heart was weak, like autumn stream

Whose source dries up in summer's heat,
Once flourishing, for all did meet
Their own desire for all that's sweet.

Who relished each draught daily drawn,
Encouraged to seek out the faun
Who danced in meadows, comes the dawn.

Who played on five pipes lovely tune.
Born of his dreams birthed by the moon
Whose circuit rising still in June

Makes great influence on stout hearts,
Who willingly give of their parts,

Once instructed in lover's arts.

To sway with emotion and verse,
To ever eschew the adverse,
To pen some verses not so terse.

Such enrich the ears that do hear,
Perform with courage, do not fear,
To foundations of love draw near.

So, that poor pair who from town fled
In mid of day from home they shed
Confines of shackles to which bred.

So freed themselves and on new path
Together trod, so fled the wrath,
And so rejoiced in aftermath.

In brightest noon or darkest night
They sang in wisdom as was right
Of all that came within their sight,

So shared through years and brought to bear
Many a lilt of sweetest air.

With all of mankind they will share

The lessons learned, the visions seen,
As did perchance appear on scene,
What better lessons could have been

Made on their journey, to them shown,
As dreams or visions by them known,
Until their love was to full grown.

Thus do recall from whence had come,
How in need of hour fled the glum,
To free themselves from under thumb.

The ropes that held, the knots that bound,
Within confines of thickset mound,
Built fast to withstand all around,

Who would resist that terror rule
Where saw each person as a tool?
Thus fled they far with piebald mule

Whose heart would burst from burden borne,
Who served them nobly until torn,

On thirteenth day, and on that morn

They dug a grave and honor gave
To weakened steed that them did save
Out from the tumult of that knave

Who now in memory grows weak
Like a whisper from far off peak,
As so quiet as mouse does squeak.

Such eyes and ears are now attuned,
Anvil, stirrup and drum heal wound,
Rebound with grace, no longer doomed.

Do from storehouse, riches of time,
From past and from future sublime,
Such visions as benefit rhyme,

To draw from stories shared before,
Recorded as from farthest shore,
Or perhaps nearby, which is more

Easily understood in word,
Even when such speech may be slurred,

Each syllable being so blurred.

The ear is able to discern,
For language akin does not burn,
Rather it soothes and so shall turn

The heart to attune to the chord,
To understand meaning of word,
To beat plowshare out from the sword.

The horse shall put end to her scream,
Poseid and Atlas then shall dream,
And all milk shall froth with sweet cream.

So peace shall like a river flow,
Anxiety flees, each will know
How true love to each other show.

Faeries

Look with me closely, what do we see,
So slight the impressions on forest floor.
The space between each shows a swift passage,
Yet what so lightly and speedily steps?

You say it is sprite, that may well be,
As the passage of glade is faerie field.
I spied an old ring, though golden it lay,
And broken and fallen from better times.

Next, not seven steps, were sweet chamomile,
Another sure witness of blessings here.
See, there on that stump some fungi rises
Fresh from the mist seeping from cedar tree.

Like blood coursing through this thriving forest,
Life teems and flourishes in faerie's trail.
Such must be who made these slight impressions;
None other can move so swiftly as these.

At such moment there came a shrill whistle
High over our heads, we thought perhaps wind.

While branches swayed deeply in deference
A cloud covered our faces, a chill came.

Then clatter of wing beating against wing.
A din was swelling and filling this glade.
Fair flutes and pipes and perhaps seven strings
Played out a melody kind to our ears.

While eyes grew heavy, deep formed our slumbers.
Low bowed our heads against soft forest floor.
Comfort so calming, like sweet willow balm,
Gave me impression I was not alone.

Though may not be sure, I believe did see
Three faeries on damselflies enter close.
Gossamer wings stretching over my head,
And voices sung softly courageous song.

Song of conquest, song of sword fighting men,
Raising their battle cries and moans as fell
Beneath long shafts raining out of the sun,
Piercing their leathers and shattering bones.

Next vision revealed was near quiet brook,

Where lapped a doe with two fresh spotted fawns.
When startled, broke quickly, flying away
Like butterflies they seemed, leaping the trees.

Soon I did awake and the mist was gone.
My companion from dim night also rose.
We stared at each other in disbelief.
Was it truly faeries deceiving us?

We know are sly and secretly desire
To cover and hide from probing as ours.
In forest glade where mushroom ring grows
And sweet chamomile fills air pleasingly.

So seek we next morning where we had been,
The ring of mushrooms, the soft impressions
At forest edge near some soft flowing stream,
Yet still hidden remains, a place of dreams.

Agonistes

Sculpting the lines requires a finely tuned eye.
Ambergris and spatula, meeting white lead,
With husks plucked until valley walnut season
Stripped bare beyond gleaning, for precious is oil,
Boiled and blackened, ambergris fragrance does tie
Image to canvas, an underlying bed,
Foundation for creation, such is reason
Such effort exerted, the payment for toil,
Exaltation, to sustain glistening lie.

Cast under shadows of artists gone before,
Looming over landscape, hidden were their notes.
So, manifest possesses us, as does fear.
Poisonous this potion concocted today,
Yet we are captured by myths, such is the lore.
The skill of those masters ventures over moats,
Barrier to castle, where treasure is dear,
By ramparts protected, yet we must hold sway,
For my finely tuned eye must bring in the score.

Melodies melt into background of Spring day.
This magician carefully attends each word.

78

Precision forestalls failure, what we create
Is short and found wanting if error is made.
To glisten is needed, to refract will pay
Rewards for ages, with resounding accord.
Each line on this canvas, laid as if by fate,
Each color sublime, will shimmer in the shade.
Success will be rewarded, and all will say

Captured is the likeness that masters create.
Here is golden triangle that all have sought.
Proportion and freedom meet beautifully.
What Greeks saw as perfection is here portrayed.
How Vermeer in windowpane did heavens make,
So accurate his eye, with skill he has wrought
Layers upon layers, each so cordially
Brings out a vision, and to this day is played
That moment he painted in studio late.

Soon this we begin, to proceed in their steps.
The formula is fixed, ambergris gives scent.
We will trap each viewer in the mystery.
This visage will haunt them throughout all of time.
More than a portrait, this will foster regrets,
Revealing to marrow, revealing the bent,

Opening wider than space across the sea.
Each thought is exposed, blatantly shows crime.
No pretense avails, as enshrine concepts.

A Maiden's Glory

If I were a fair young maiden,
One who's hair flowed golden and free,
How many beaus would seek my hand
To cherish and fill me with glee.

If my lips were like the ruby,
Sought after like some treasure store,
Courtiers would come a courting,
My delights to fully explore.

Were my thighs like freshly stirred cream,
Or my feet nimble and dainty,
Could men be drawn to seek me out,
Even though live in this shanty.

I spied a young man over Christmas,
He held an axe ever so fair,
As felled that fir, I considered that,
His fists would sorely crush my hair.

That I find not acceptable,
For my hair is as precious as gold.

Yet not by strength or binding knot
Will I suffer my treasure be sold.

Father does seek a good bride price,
He hopes to produce an heir.
I'll not be bartered like fattened pig
That is offered at Kensington Fair.

There is one young man I desire;
He has hopes for me also.
If only he wasn't poorer than me,
Perhaps we could make it a go.

We could put two kettles together,
He has one from his mother, I know.
I can steal the one over our hearth.
Perhaps my father won't know.

We would travel as far as London town
Or perhaps to Scarborough, fair.
With two trusty pots on our backs,
And me, with my gold flowing hair.

All would be as sweet as honey,
Each day without ever a care.
My young man and I, we would cherish
Our love and my long golden hair.

Among Giants

Among giants we wander, gaunt, awestruck.
Aged though we are, they are much older,
And bolder also, bearing against buck
Offered up by winter's wind, and colder

Than is our accustomed piedmont season,
Twenty-four experienced, like water
Filling up creek beds, where washed rocks glisten,
And river otter and belt kingfisher

Oft visited that realm, replenished glen,
Where wedding bells charged, canticle warning,
Heed vows taken, temper venal heathen,
Who as a weed in garden patch growing

Requires attention to prevent illness
From days after creation, after sin
Broke into pure world, birthing such duress,
That even giants clamor under wind.

Such were the dreams taken, rivers flowing
Frozen in summer, so out of reason,

Turned from purpose, are these giants knowing,
Seeing ages groaning out of season.

Hollow at their core, they blister and break,
Sound heart has hastened to harvester's store.
Dropping as mayflies, what more can they take,
And we watch, awestruck, so gaunt and much more.

Aged we are, and yet aged shall be
If we greet many more years on this earth;
Yet shall attain not the stature of these,
These noble giants, girth nurtured since birth.

That since hundreds of years outlast mankind,
Who lives a season, sustaining his way,
By rhyme or reason, and soundness of mind,
Yet to dust must return, there's no other way.

Thus, what choice do we have but be awestruck.
We wander mindless of measure of time.
What thoughts are our own, are we so moonstruck
That darkness is light, and life has no rhyme.

Aged as we are, why should they count years?

These trees neither sorrow, nor in turmoil
Remember seasons, as we do the tears.
Each will diminish and triumphant soil

Will receive back what generously gave;
Will welcome these giants and the dreamers,
Though hollow or gaunt, no longer are slave
To perdition that reigns since black schemers.

Free are the visions, free are the clear dreams,
Like swallows in Spring, they wing higher still:
Rejoice as the ostrich, swift as wind streams.
Each flies higher in ether than Enlil

Who Sumerians in fear bowed down to:
Imagining that such statue could hear,
Where sunset met the western sea so blue
And softer breeze would so tickle each ear,

That thinking of want or thinking of pain,
Were far from their pondering, all seemed well,
Counted not cost, refused writing that came,
So fell in oblivion, who can tell

Their generation, passed swiftly, no more
Shall people rejoice in riches that spoil,
As rust ruins iron, all reach that door,
The end of all things, return to the soil.

Cassia and Lorenzo

At the western edge flows a mythic stream
Fed by spring deep underground, she's pining
For Lorenzo, who she knows, will not return.
Her tears feed the stream so incessantly,
Whose waters are clear as run over stones
Stones washed in sadness reveal lovers true
To each other despite separation.

Lorenzo was her rock, her strength in life;
Solid as true granite, dark as moonless night,
Birthed in mountains among Firenze goatherds.
Known to be faithful and true from his youth,
Like a whispering wind, like sweet honey.
Soothing his speech, and would his presence bring
Calm restoration to long enemies.

Cassia, born of richest family,
Royal through heritage, destined to be,
Her eyes would with each sunrise reflecting
Glisten in that mirror, so clearly see
Sorrow in future, endless eves, and mourns
That she is bound to promise parents made,

Wed to a prince of Constantinople.

Woe is inheritance given lovers,
Crossed among stars of dim constellations.
Tormented in universe for endless time,
Cast aside are the comforts, facing fate,
To tumble and stumble, falter and fail,
Selecting each stone as beneficial.
Hardships would face together for all time.

Cast as by sculptor, their forms intertwined,
Hands grasping hands in wondrous embracing.
Curious, their hearts discovered that eve,
Secrets best kept for only each other,
Shared in the moments of morning lark song.
Too late is departure from delight's bed,
Waking to warning as entered through door,

Judgement would fall swiftly from father's hand.
Anger did rage through hallways, though fleeing
Lorenzo was captured by garden stream.
Portico for eternal destiny,
Stone struck his temple as fell mortally
Wounded, and then Cassia was swooning,

89

Fell to the stones, and her tears were welling.

As tales are related, sad tales of love,
On west edge, Cassia, like faithful dove,
Washes stones daily, lovers living still,
Faithful always as caress stones with tears.
What better reminder, wishing on stars,
Their momentary lives burst on our sight,
Testimony that crossed love shall be dashed.

Spenserian Reversal

His bowels quiver as does consider such night's end,
What squirming shall profit, what shall forfend
These visions reveal such suffering, pain,
In consequence of choices by orphaned
Child from Hanover grown up under rain-
Soaked cardboard containers behind a chain
Linked fence, set behind broken building,
Beneath the A train that incessantly came
To break through his nightmares, as a gelding,

Gives over to castration consent to power,
Such cunning corruption taken that hour.
Whose purpose is served, whose benefit comes?
This method, such madness, like a glower
Facing fecundity, brittle as crumbs
Left on floor from morning meal, when beat drums
along Mohawk that continue to beat
Message unheeded unless toothache numbs
Away all senses and with them replete

Are protestations, each one regarded close friend
Clasped to his chest tightly, called to attend,

His ramblings, his mishegoss, observed by all.
In their assembly he never did blend
In Yonkers yeshiva, and there in that hall
With each of the students daily did brawl
Over each meaning of words in scriptures
Scanned in the Talmud, he had chutzpah, gaul
to question the rabbi, damn the strictures.

Placed over his head, the yellow yarmelke worn,
Like symbol of rejection, like a corn
That resists all attempts at removal,
No medicament serves, it must be borne
Like mark of Cain denotes disapproval
For deed of death, the first foul removal
Of kindred blood so shed in jealousy,
Long days in past still meets his approval
As he values same animosity

That he never releases, so will never mend,
The wounds would be scars that should he attend.
Through noxious night seasons, so he should deign,
Grant self some respite, in place of this rend.
And stop slaughtering moment, to refrain
From impetus set in motion, such pain

Has not ceased, thus he weeps, wilting
Like peonies in heat, after brief rain
Do strangle themselves, so he is tilting.

What Dreams Are Made Of

Had I known it was a perilous day,
I would have thought twice before leaving bed.
Had I known I was about to stumble,
I would have thought better to stay in bed.
Had I known the bruises and elbow scrapes,
I would have thought, "Am I wise to leave bed?"
Had I known that I would seek to move limbs,
I would have thought, "Should leave forest, not bed."
In bed where ground is soft and receiving,
In bed where stab deep the fallen branches,
In bed with the winter flora growing,
In bed, I won't know it, I'll keep snoring.

So wrapped in my dreams, like in envelope,
The colors are vibrant, and changes each.
How the plot ties together I don't know,
I was in a car, then on bicycle
Riding over road, towards Yosemite.
Yet, that swiftly morphed into widest sea.
My ship was adrift, and then suddenly
I was back on bus to Bratislava.
My two boys beside me, we were flat broke

Knew that the conductor would ask for fare.
Must be like the gypsies, and take light bulbs.
So coach becomes dark, and we can then hide,
But daylight has come, and it matters not,
For the bus became a cart and careens
Swiftly down hill, the brakes do not function.
We fly through the air as on Ferris wheel
In Donau Zentrum, this time with tickets.
The skyline is lavender with the sun.
Some music comes wafting like cold air,
Icicles form at the end of my nose.
At once I am transported back to bed.
My foot has a cramp, it is right twisted.
The pain surpasses dreams that had held me,
I have no choice, I must get out of bed.

Had I known that foot cramp would waken me,
I would have thought to drink some more water.
Had I known that a foot cramp would shake me,
I would have set alarm, to drink water.
Had I known that two feet would so stumble,
I would have reconsidered what to do.
Instead of moving branches from forest,
Instead of breaking branches in forest,

Instead of tromping, and dragging them down,
Instead of watching where my feet touched ground,
Instead my foot struck under broken limb,
Instead I took tumble and scraped my skin.

Again I lay in bed, waiting for sleep.
My pillows are puffed up, my sheets are soft.
Scrape at my elbow reminds me of loss
Of balance I suffered, when tripped over
That broken limb I had noticed, but still
Had not picked it up to avert danger.
Had ignored the warning that my eyes saw,
So focused on dragging branches away.
Determined to take more branches than safe,
Took limbs in both left and right hands, so that
I was not watching where I placed my feet.
That limb I had avoided leapt at me,
Grasping my left foot, sending me tumbling
Across forest floor, and onto pavement.
Tumbling and skidding, scraping both my hands,
Sweater was wearing gave little safety.
As I landed not softly, rather hard,
Yet, my head was not injured, that is good.
More hurt was my pride, for surely had failed

To provide for my safety, as I should.
Careless, brings danger, I should be aware,
For this is not first time I have stumbled.
I am long past the age, bones break with ease.
So must watch myself, "Please be careful, please."

Had I known it was a perilous day,
I would have thought twice before leaving dreams.
Had I known I was about to stumble,
I would have thought better to stay asleep.
Had I known the bruises and elbow scrapes,
I would have thought, "Better to stay in dreams."

Beyond Samothrakikós Shores

Grasses grow tall, tilting across Gallipoli
Towards Samothraki, fairer on sea.
Unlike peninsula, this isle is peacefully
Descent from sailors, who happily
Meet on crystal beaches, make life musically
In bright raiment for festivity.
Remember their forefathers, honor memory,
Gather their nets, recount history
Of each glass blown float, recovered from middle sea,
Green or blue, some drawn from olive tree.
For inspiration, here eternally, as free,
As for ages, immortally,
From Olympus once drew their own insurgency.
As on that Mount, gods incessantly
Found reasons to foster hourly calamity.
Like bickering children who would plea
Between parents who argue and choose carelessly.
Shall Priam or Agamemnon flee,
Will Ajax prevail, will Paris with Helen see
Walls of Troy prevail, bring victory?
Or shall Hera on Olympus in fervency
Prevail over fair Persephone?

Whose mother she hated, would show no courtesy,
For daughter, like mother, cheerfully
Flaunted her beauty, and such beauty so gaily
Could so easily prompt destiny.
Tyche, the daughter of Zeus and Aphrodite,
On behalf of Hellas argosy,
Once plied for profit, now for warfare fearlessly
Crossed sea towards Troy, without harmony.
For between the leaders grew animosity,
Why lone bride should bring calamity,
So argued soldiers while crossing sea.
Who noble Achilles persuaded, did not see,
His end was in clouds, so artlessly
Driven by rash Hera, though animosity, Aimed towards his
foes, who ever should flee
When his mien turned against them, such absurdity,
That he might meet defeat. Enmity
Burned in heart of Zeus who Hera had so tirelessly
Annoyed with subterfuge, willingly
Played favorite hero as fool, purposefully
Brought him to Troy, then incessantly
Annoyed better graces, breaching fraternity.
Required persuasion, with Phoenix, three
Warriors met Achilles to bind, apparently

To swear for battle, to bend his knee
Under command of leaders of Hellas who he
Despised and decried, yet like fair tree
Yields fruit of olive whose oil shines faces with glee,
He forged into battle, all could see
His face glisten with brightness, his eyes mistily
Filling with sorrows that such beastly
And ruinous squabble over bride who did flee
With fair lover, Paris equally,
Or more at fault for his actions, contemptibly
Stole love when should have stayed assignee
Of peace delegation, to promote and appease.
Ignoring brother, stole across sea,
Such love did appeal to his youth more robustly.
So hid he Helen, brought apogee
Of father's kingdom, as Troy fell in history.
Betrayed by whims, Olympians see
Their machinations, while Hellenes do swear madly.
From homes have been forced, left apple and olive tree,
Their fruit will fail, on plains beside sea.
Which should never have crossed, what profit a devotee
Gains from gods of warfare, who like flea
Cares not for each victim from whose blood drinks freely.
So those who dwell on Olympus see

Their minions of earth who willingly, ceaselessly
Die for no purpose, yet willingly
Charge into pitch battle, as on Gallipoli,
Where now grasses grow so peacefully,
Tilting toward shores of Samothraki.

Journey Home

Along bluebell highway, in west Texas,
On the way to Roswell, across red earth,
One lane west, the only one to my birth,
Pinyon in the Guadalupe, vexes.
We harvested seeds for many a meal,
Gathered from the cones Scrub Jays did not steal.

Those Pinyons stressed us in our chiminea,
Fire much too hot, it did scorch our flat bread.
I am not much good at cooking, I've said.
Cooking was easy, back in Korea.
We had moved there, back in nineteen fifty,
Away from land of birth, among scrub tree.

We must defend for freedom, that was call.
We moved, as some families did, with their men.
Support the troops, more important, for then
Red Menace was expanding over all.
A line must be drawn in sand, even if not,
Rather in mountains, that the war was fought.

Little I remember from those few years:

The shouts of "Retreat!", the mountain afire,
My arm, searing hot, from enemy fire.
A medic appeared, I held back my tears.
Wanted to fight, yet couldn't pull trigger;
Taken from the field, how might they figure

I could ever return to the front line.
Bones had been shattered, muscles had been torn.
To save arm, impossible, so forlorn
I woke in a tent, constructed with twine.
A one armed man, still, I was alive.
Came from the battlefield, I did survive.

Was good it is left, the one I did lose.
So, in coming years, as learn how to shift
With one arm and two feet, avoiding drift,
As change gears, going downhill, which to choose:
From fourth to third, then from third to second,
Earlier years, I had not so reckoned.

I drift through Roswell as the sun does set.
Store signs remind me of years from my youth.
F. W. Woolworth's, so much a truth.
Spent youth there, at counter, sodas to get,

103

Served as root beer, with vanilla ice cream.
Each day after school, would sit there, a dream

Like no other, for gone was my sorrow.
As I sat there, looking in the mirror,
No father I saw, I saw no terror.
Good for today, better for tomorrow,
Better to have him away, out my life,
Better to avoid, many tears and strife.

Perhaps that is why I signed up for war.
With young wife and children, unprepared, so
When bullet struck, lost arm below elbow.
My wife and my children gave out a roar
Of joy, that I was alive, though crippled.
We took my arm, then did have it pickled.

We stored it in jar for the journey home,
A raggedy reminder of the war
To never forget, to hold freedom's door
Firm as we can, though across ocean's foam
Our interest extends, around the earth
May freedom resound, right given by birth.

It should not matter where person is born,
Nor color of skin, as God has given
Life to us all, as a gift from Heaven.
Pursuit of happiness, not to be torn
Or shredded by despots, or governments,
Instituted to care, not collect rents.

I have an opinion, and don't care,
If neighbors find me weird or unsightly.
I will still act the same, I'll do rightly
By them, as my brothers, be sure to share
What have of resources, blessings of life
Have been given to me, along with wife.

Roswell now lies more than ten miles behind.
The dust on my window, it now cakes thick.
Red earth is blessing, if it won't stick,
Blinding my vision, as road now does wind
Up through the Guadalupe, dry as bone.
Like skeleton left to dry, hard as stone.

Soon, as the high pass comes into my view,
I know am near home, my heart lightens some.
The weights I have carried, oh, so tiresome,

Shall soon be forgotten, as I pass through
A cocoon covering, a temple gate
Opens before me, I am not too late.

Protection I find, away from the storm.
The world left behind, like forgotten dream
That troubled my sleep, yet, now it does seem
Has vanished, like mist, on hot sultry morn.
So, refreshed I can sit, in the sun's rays,
Glad to have purpose, and free from malaise.

As I pull up to end of our fence line
Where Six Pinyon Pine stand guard at the gate,
My cares they are jettisoned, as dead weight.
My shoulders relax, and so does my mind,
At home I have peace, the world with its cares
Ends at my fence line, some others' affairs.

Yet, I am not vagrant in thoughts towards them.
I plow and I plant each spring, to attend
To needs of my family, I amend
Soil to make fertile, good as diadem
In crown of agent who provides good rule,
As scepter of Wenceslas, played in school.

These memories are like treasures I store:
Some good, some bad, as most people do know.
I have put them down here before I go
Away from this earth. Neither rich nor poor,
I have seen a life, beyond good measure.
And bequeath some lines, my only treasure.

www.ingramcontent.com/pod-product-compliance
Lightning Source LLC
Chambersburg PA
CBHW072357090426
42741CB00012B/3068